6.95

GREAT SCIENCE
FAIR PROJECTS

A

5-4

GREAT SCIENCE FAIR PROJECTS

PHYLLIS KATZ AND JANET FREKKO

ILLUSTRATIONS BY PAUL HARVEY

FRANKLIN WATTS
NEW YORK / LONDON / TORONTO / SYDNEY

First Paperback Edition 1992

Library of Congress Cataloging-in-Publication Data

Katz, Phyllis, 1946–
    Great science fair projects / by Phyllis Katz and Janet Frekko.
       p.   cm.
    Includes bibliographical references and index.
    Summary: Suggestions for science fair projects, with information
on collecting data and displaying the final result.
    ISBN 0-531-11015-X (lib. ed.)—ISBN 0-531-15628-1 (pbk.)
    1. Science projects—Juvenile literature.   2. Science—
Exhibitions—Juvenile literature.   [1. Science projects.
2. Science—Exhibitions.]   I. Frekko, Janet.   II. Title.
Q182.3.K36   1992
507′.B—dc20   91-17299 CIP AC

TO OUR
HUSBANDS, VICTOR AND GENE,
AND TO THE WONDERFUL
"COLD SPAGHETTI GANG"

CONTENTS

GREAT SCIENCE
FAIR PROJECTS

WELCOME TO THE FAIR!

Have you been to a county fair? A state fair? A crafts fair? What do you think you'll see?

You'll find row after row of booths. Each booth space will have people showing you something they've done. Sometimes you will see an animal that someone has raised. You may see a special quilt pattern that someone has worked on for a year. Maybe you'll get to see (and taste) a prize-winning jam or jelly recipe.

Whatever the subject, each booth displays some kind of work. The people at the booth are proud of what they've done, and most of them have had a lot of fun doing it. They like to talk about their work and tell you how they got interested in it, the stories that happened along the way, and what they found out.

A science fair is your chance to be a part of all this fun in your own school.

You can

- choose something that is interesting to you.
- think about your topic.
- find out what other people have thought about it.
- do an experiment yourself or with friends or family.
- be at the fair itself and show people your project.

It feels good to think and give your brain exercise, just as it feels good to use your muscles when you run, ride a bicycle, or play on a team. Doesn't it feel great to solve a puzzle, too?

Science is full of puzzles. Some of the puzzles were worked out many years ago and have become what we call science "facts" and "theories." All of us try one way and then another to solve a problem. Scientists do this in a special way with experiments.

HOW DO WE LEARN TO USE A SPOON?

Have you ever watched a baby try to use a spoon for the first time? It's funny. The baby wants the food on the spoon and knows that the mouth is how you get it in. But it takes some practice to use the arm and the hand, scoop up the food, and aim it right into the mouth. It's a mess at first. There may be applesauce on the baby's cheeks, neck, and hair—all over the place. But after a while, babies do learn to use spoons. They do experiments by *trial and error.*

Trying first one way and then another is an important part of living and an important part of science. We all do experiments to learn how to survive in the world. Some things we have to learn ourselves—like using a spoon. We can also learn about the experiments other people have done, sometimes many years before we came along. That method is called doing *research.*

Research can be

- reading about other people's experiments.
- doing an activity that repeats what other people did.
- watching a demonstration or an exhibit.
- listening to someone talk about an idea.
- setting up your own experiments.

Doing something yourself gives you a chance to use your eyes, your ears, your nose, your mouth, your mind, and your hands. The more of these senses you use, the better your information will be and the more you will learn.

SCIENTIFIC METHOD

A science experiment is different from that baby learning how to eat with a spoon. The baby uses trial and error to solve the problem and doesn't think about how much food is on the spoon, how long the handle is, or whether the food is sticky or soupy.

Scientists set up experiments to look at the way *one* thing works. That is the *variable*—the thing that varies or changes when other things in the experiment stay the same, or are *controlled*. They guess what they think will happen, and that is their *hypothesis*. A real experiment is a good mystery. You think you know what will happen, but you might be surprised. Your curiosity keeps you going. Your brain "itches," and it feels good to "scratch" it.

Look around you. Who found a way to make sound travel through wires? What experiments were done to make a medicine that prevents you from coughing so that you can sleep through the night? How did someone think about putting pictures on tape so that they would run through your VCR? Scientists and inventors asked these questions and carefully looked for answers. Sometimes they were surprised, and the surprises were useful.

The experiments in this book are not hard to do, but there are no "right" answers. You will find out what happens when you use certain things at certain times and with certain controls. If you are careful when you set up an experiment, you will get an answer to your question. Often, the hardest part of science is knowing what questions to ask.

We chose the questions in this book so that you could use the things that are all around you and get some experience in the way scientists answer their questions. We also chose them because they don't need expensive materials or a lot of adult help.

We hope you wonder about everything around you. As you wonder, you will dream up your own experiments. Maybe you will think about becoming a scientist. Or maybe you'll just be a better shopper, or baker, or painter because you found out something you didn't know before.

A NOTE ON SAFETY

If you like experimenting and inventing, remember to think about safety. Do you know enough to understand what your invention might do as you work on it or when you're finished? Think of others. Will your experiment or invention make a funny smell or a lot of noise? Where should you do these things? This is when it's good to do some research and ask a teacher or other adult.

COLLECTING DATA

When you are interested in observing something and telling other people about it, you must first form a question. Your statement of what you think will happen is your hypothesis. For example, if you wonder how much the grass grows in your neighborhood in a summer month, your hypothesis could be "The grass on the south side of the park grows 3 inches (7.62 cm) in July."

You then set up your procedures as a way of answering your question. You'll want to observe carefully, collect your information, and then think about it. You may have to ask the park maintenance people to leave a patch unmowed for your experiment. When you've finished your project, you'll want to present your information to other people to tell them what you think and to see what they have to say.

THE "LEGWORK" OF SCIENCE

You will be best at convincing people that your hypothesis is true or not true by giving them the pieces of information you have observed. These pieces of information are called *data*. Collecting data is the daily work of scientists, who then use their special talent to figure out what it means. This is called *interpreting data*.

What does it mean if the grass you have measured grows 1 inch (2.5 cm) instead of the 3 you hypothesized? Did someone forget to water it? Is it a slow-growing type? Has it got a disease? Maybe you didn't know enough about that type of grass to make a good guess. Aha! Now, what do you think? There's a new puzzle to solve. In science, one puzzle often leads to another.

Scientists work at interpreting data. An interpretation that has lots of data from experiments used to test many variables (one at a time) can lead to a theory that helps us understand how our world works. Every little piece of data helps form a whole picture, just like the pieces of a puzzle.

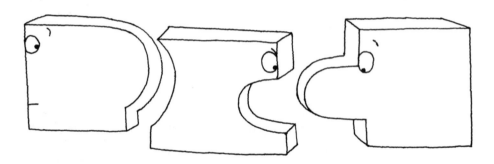

THE MANY FORMS
OF DATA

Those pieces of information, or data, come in many forms. The beautiful drawings of North American birds by John James Audubon (1785–1851) are data on the shape, size, and color of those birds. Benjamin Banneker (1731–1806) watched the stars and published an almanac as data. Marie Curie (1867–1934) measured the strength and effects of radioactivity and with her husband, Pierre, began the modern studies in nuclear chemistry in the laboratory.

Your data can be in the form of drawings, photographs, sound recordings, lists, charts, graphs, or samples.

Before you start your experiment, you need to think about something called *sample size*. The sample size is the part (or sample) of what you are looking at in your experiment and are using as an example of everything of that type. Let's say you want to see how many cars stop at your corner stop sign. How many cars would you have to watch and check off to say that nine out of ten cars stop at the sign? If you look at one car, can you say that "all" or even "many" or "most" of the cars coming to the corner will do the same thing? The larger your sample size, the surer you can be that what you are seeing is what is usually there.

There is no magic number for sample size. You do want enough data to convince someone else that what you found out is true. That's the reason working scientists talk and write about their work—they explain their data to each other.

You can also make some interesting discoveries when strange or unusual things pop up. But how will you know what's usual and what's unusual unless you have enough data?

MEASUREMENT

Scientists often study a question by setting up their experiments carefully with one variable (one thing that changes) and by doing lots of measurement and recording. They want to collect enough data to convince themselves that they are really testing only one variable. They want to be sure the test gives the same results when run again and again using the same conditions. This makes the test *reliable*. Scientists feel that they have done a good job when other scientists can use their exact experiments and get the same answer.

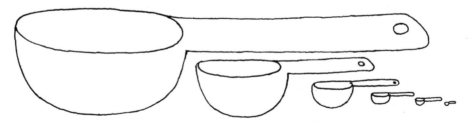

Measuring is an important part of science because differences in measurement tell us how something changes. If you see that there are no changes when you do an experiment, that is data, too.

You have probably seen measuring cups, measuring spoons, marks on baby bottles, and medicine spoons. You have certainly seen clocks. These are all measuring *standards*. That means that we all agree that every cup of flour is the same size and that a minute is a certain amount of time. That wasn't always the case.

SYSTEMS OF WEIGHTS AND MEASURES

You know that before the United States was an independent country it was a collection of English colonies following English rules. The rules for weighing and measuring things were not firmly set in England, so they were not firmly set in the colonies. This was especially confusing in business. Could you buy the same amount of flour in a bag in Boston, Massachusetts, as you could in Richmond, Virginia? How could you make business fair?

It wasn't until 1830, when the United States had been independent for over forty years, that the Senate passed a resolution asking the secretary of the treasury to study measurement standards. In 1832, the units of measurement were decided. It is not a surprise that they used the names and ideas that came from England: inches, yards, and miles for distance; quarts, bushels, and gallons for liquid volume, and so on. In this system, there are 36 inches in a yard and 4 quarts in a gallon. The reasons for these particular numbers are buried deep in history.

The metric, or decimal, system uses the meter for distance and the kilogram for mass. The system comes to us from France. The Paris Academy of Sciences reported its studies on this measurement system, based on the number 10, to the French government in 1791. The French government accepted these standards, which had first been suggested over a hundred years earlier. It can take a long time for scientists to get their ideas accepted. Most of the world uses the metric system now.

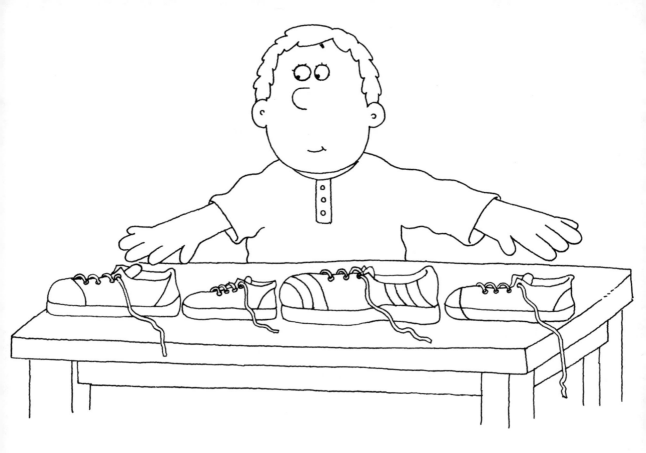

TIPS ON MEASUREMENT

When you measure, be careful. Watch your measurement marks on spoons, cups, test tubes, or scales. Keep the tops of spoonfuls and cupfuls level. Remember, you want other people to be able to understand and repeat what you do.

You can do science experiments even if you don't have standard measuring equipment; just describe what you are using and use it with care the same way each time. Let's say you don't have a ruler. You could use a "sneaker length," but you would have to report what brand, size, and model so that everyone would know what you were talking about. Using standard measures, most people will understand you without any added descriptions. Standard measures help us understand each other better.

Measuring and recording data are important techniques for solving your science mystery, no matter how small. In a science fair project, you not only get to solve the mystery, you get to decide what mystery it will be!

DISPLAYING YOUR PROJECT

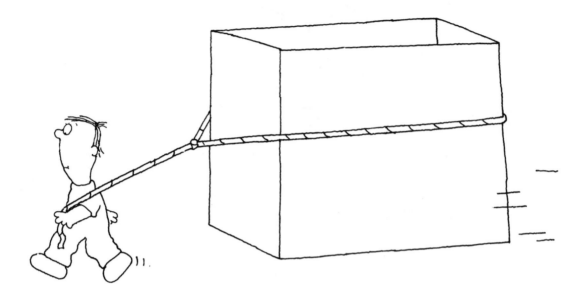

Before you decide how to display your project, make sure that you know any requirements or limitations at your school. Fairs differ from school to school. Some schools have very specific requirements and dimensions for displays; some leave that up to you. Check it out.

- Does your display need to be able to stand by itself, or will you have a wall to lean it against?
- Can it be any size?
- How much space will you be given?
- How will you take it to school?
- How much money do you want to spend?

A very inexpensive way to create a freestanding backdrop is to use a large piece of corrugated cardboard, such as a washing machine box or a TV box—or if you want it really big, a refrigerator box. Many appliance stores will save these for you if you call ahead.

TWO- OR THREE-PIECE DISPLAY

Ask an adult to cut off two or three sides of the box for you to use. You can use two or three pieces of the cardboard and hinge them together with masking tape for a display. (Plastic display hinges can be purchased at art supply stores.) If you don't like brown, you can always cover it or paint it with tempera.

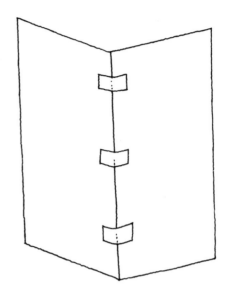

ONE-PIECE DISPLAY

Another option is to use one large piece of cardboard and score (scratch a line on) it to create a single backdrop with two side pieces. For easy transporting, the two side pieces should be half as wide as the back so that it will fold flat. Make sure that the cardboard is cut straight. Measure the width of the cardboard. Divide that number by 4, and measure from the left edge of the cardboard that number of inches toward the middle. Mark with a pencil. Do that three more times down the side of the cardboard so that you will have three marks in a line. Place a straightedge (yardstick or meter stick) along the marks, and draw a straight line. Do the same from the right edge of the cardboard. Ask an adult to score those lines with a sharp edge such as the edge of a pair of scissors. Do not cut all the way through. Fold those scored flaps toward the middle. Stand your display up.

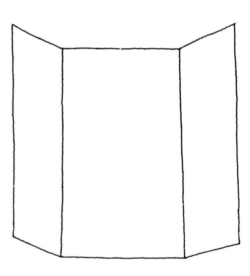

The same type of display can be made using ¼-inch (0.625-cm) foam core board that can be purchased at art supply stores. This will give you a white background.

Prefolded, heavy-duty display boards well suited for science fair projects can be purchased from Showboard, P.O. Box 10656, Tampa, FL 33679-0656.

You can also construct wooden frames and hinge them together with metal hinges, but that can be expensive, too. Poster board can then be attached to the frame. Make sure the frames are the same size or half the size (outside dimension) of the poster board so that everything will fit. If your school has a science fair every year, a wooden frame may not be a bad investment. You can change the posters every year but keep the same frame.

WRITING THE WORDS

Find out the rules at your school. Generally, the title is made large so that everyone can see from a distance what your project is. Does your school want you to state your question and hypothesis? How about results? How much detail is expected? Be clear and concise. You want your visitors to be able to see quickly what your project is about. For details, however, they will need to look at your data or report.

Drawings, photographs, charts, and graphs add to the appearance and let visitors know that you understand what you are doing. Write everything on a separate piece of paper and glue or tape it to your backdrop. If you mess up, you won't have to go out and make another background.

Part One

TAKE A CLOSER LOOK

MAKING CUT FLOWERS LAST

What about? Have you ever wondered about ways to make cut flowers last longer? Is it better to use warm or cold water? Is it better to cut the stems underwater? Is it better to cut the stems at an angle to expose more surface area? Are there things that can be added to the water that help?

What's your guess?

Here's one way: Ask at least ten people what they do to make cut flowers last longer. Call a florist. Make a list of the various ways that people keep cut flowers fresh. In a science book or encyclopedia look up "plants" to find out how water moves inside them.

How do you begin to test? Use only one kind of plant. A daisy or similar flower would be good. Set up a chart to keep track of the things you are testing, such as the following:

Number of Days without Wilting	Cold Water	Warm Water	Cut under Water	Cut in Air	Cut Straight Across	Cut at 45° angle	Preservative Added to the Water
Day 1							
Day 2							
Day 3							
Day 4							

What you'll need: Flowers, containers, water, scissors.

Have you thought about? What happens when you combine various procedures? Cut at angle *and* cold water?

What did you find out?

Now, what would happen if? Will the best preservation method for daisies work for other flowers?

Going to the fair. Take your raw data. Original records are very important. It shows that you did the work over a period of time. Take with you some cut flowers that show the various methods of preservation used.

HOW MUCH SALT?

What about? We have all been told that too much salt isn't good for our bodies. Our bodies, however, must have *some* salt. Which foods contain a lot of salt? How would you go about finding out which foods contain a lot of salt?

What do the experts say? How much salt does your body need? How much is too much? What can too much salt do to your body?

What's your guess? How much salt is contained in various foods?

Here's one way: Take ½ cup of a salty food, such as potato chips or salted peanuts, and pour in the same amount of water. Stir. Strain the liquid and catch the liquid in a shallow container such as a cake pan or pie pan. Let the liquid evaporate. What do you have left? Salt crystals? How much—½ teaspoon? More? Less?

How do you know whether you have salt? Could it be sugar or something else?

Have you thought about? Some foods may have a lot of salt, but you didn't consider them because they don't taste particularly salty. The next time you go to the supermarket, read some labels. The ingredients are listed in order from the most to the least. Take a long hard look at cereals and canned foods. You may be surprised.

Going to the fair: This is a real opportunity to educate people about the dangers of too much salt. You can also encourage people to read the labels on the food they are buying. Demonstrate your evaporation activity and also have various foods there with labels for visitors to read. Especially good to use are the foods that have a lot more salt than people realized.

A "MEATY ISSUE"

What about? You hear about "low fat" products in ads for food. Is your lunch meat high or low in fat?

Did you know? Sausages and lunch meats are made by chopping up meat, adding spices and chemicals (usually lots of salt) to keep them fresh, and stuffing the mashed meat into a casing. This casing is often the large intestine of an animal. For many years, butchers made their own sausages and put bits and pieces of different meats into them for their own special recipe or flavor. Do you know what's in your lunch meat?

What's your guess? How much fat is there in a slice of turkey, regular bologna, or salami?

Why does it matter? You need some fats in your food to give your body energy, to make it easy to move, and for shape. But fats also can clog up your blood and make it hard for the blood to move around your body like a healthy river. People want to know how much fat is in the food they eat so that they can balance their diets and eat a healthy diet.

Here's one way: Buy packaged lunch meat—turkey, bologna, salami—that comes in 1-ounce (28-g) slices. They should all be equal so that this can be an easy experiment to control. Take a 1-quart (0.95-liter) pot and measure 2 cups (0.47 liter) of water into it. Under the supervision of an adult, put one slice of meat in and boil the water for 15 minutes. Do you see any fat floating in it? Turn it off and let it cool down. When the fat hardens, you can measure it by weight if you have a gram scale (ask at school), or you can measure it by volume. Hint: Some of the fat will stick to the bottom of your piece of meat; scrape it off and add it to the fat you collected from the cooled water. Use measuring spoons to see whether you have collected 1/4 teaspoon, 1/2 teaspoon, 1 tablespoon, or whatever amount.

Have you thought about? Controls: Did you clean the pot after each try? Was the heat the same each time you cooked the meat? Would more (or less) cooking time make a difference?

What did you find out? Data:

Type of Meat	Amount of Fat (Weight or Volume)

Now, what would happen if? Do you think different brands of meat have different amounts of fat? What about hamburger meat? What about fruits and vegetables?

Going to the fair: Ask your visitors to guess the amount of fat in the meats, and place fresh pieces of meat in zip-top plastic bags on your display. (The meat might spoil and smell during your fair, so use the bags to keep the odor inside.) Have a sample of the fat that cooked out. Which fat came from which meat? If you tried this experiment with hamburger, fruits, and vegetables, you'll have a lot of things to compare and show.

"CARS, CARS, AND MORE CARS"

What about? How many cars are on your street at a certain time of day? What car color seems to be the most popular?

Did you know? There are about 180 million cars, trucks, and buses on the streets of the United States.

What's your guess? How much traffic is there in a half hour on your street? What color are most of the cars?

Why does it matter? Is there a lot of traffic in your neighborhood? A wide street can handle more cars than a narrow street can. The color of a car can have something to do with safety. Dark cars are harder to see at night. Light cars may be harder to see during the day. Let's find out which cars are on the road near you.

Here's one way: Make up a chart to collect your raw data. It might look like the one below. Then take a pen or pencil and stand on the sidewalk next to the street you want to study. The more days you do this, the more strongly you can say what is true for that street.

Have you thought about? Controls: Are you observing at the same time each day that you count? Are you observing on both good-weather and bad-weather days?

What did you find out? Data:

Number of Cars of Each Color

Time	Date	Blue	Red	Black	White

Now, what would happen if? Is your corner like others? How different is the traffic a street or two away?

Going to the fair: Photographs of your street would be helpful here. Once you see the pattern of your data, you could display it with small model cars. For example, if there are three blue cars for every red one, you could show that with models.

BIRDS OF A FEATHER

What about? What birds live in your area? What birds like which food? Which are ground feeders? Which prefer a raised feeder?

What's your guess?

Find out about: Birds in your area. There are many good books to help you identify birds. Learn all you can about several birds that you see often near your home. From your research, which of these birds eat seeds?

Here's one way: Test which kinds of seeds birds prefer. Which birds eat from the ground? Which birds like a raised feeder?

Buy three kinds of birdseed. It may be less expensive for you to purchase a package of mixed seed if you don't mind separating the seeds into like kinds.

Test one kind of seed at a time by placing some seed on the ground and some of the same kind on a raised feeder. Watch for several days, and record what happens. (It may take a while for the birds to find your feeder.) Note which birds come to eat the first kind of seed, then remove that kind. Try Seed 2 for several days, then Seed 3.

Do the same kinds of birds like one seed better than another? You could use a chart like the one below for each kind of seed. The name of the seed could be used instead of giving each seed a number.

What did you find out? Data:

Date	Names of Birds That Eat Seed 1 from the Ground	Names of Birds That Eat Seed 1 from a Raised Feeder	Names of Birds That Eat Seed 1 from Both the Ground and the Feeder	Notes

Repeat this chart for Seed 2 and Seed 3.

What you'll need: Books about birds, three different kinds of seeds, trays or feeders.

Going to the fair: Take your original records. Drawings or photos of the birds you studied would be good. Take samples of the various seeds. Let people guess which birds like which seeds.

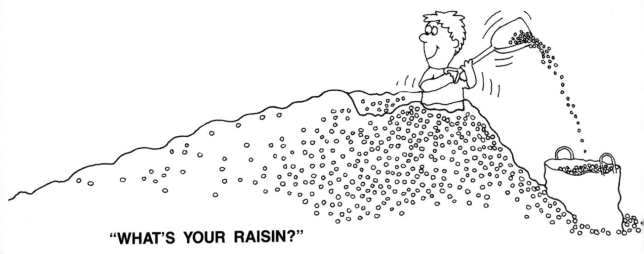

"WHAT'S YOUR RAISIN?"

What about? When plump, juicy grapes are dried out, we call them by another name: raisins. How much water does a grape lose to get its new name?

Did you know? Some grapes are raised for eating just as they are. Some are made into juice or wine, and some are raised just for drying into raisins. Different types of grapes are used for each purpose. Just for the fun of it, can you guess how many pounds of grapes were grown this year to be dried and sold as raisins? How would you find out if your guess was close?

What's your guess? How many ounces of raisins will you get if you dry out 1 pound (0.45 kg) of grapes? How does this compare to other fruits?

Why does it matter? You want to be a good shopper and save your family money. Grapes are usually a good buy in the summer, when they ripen in our country. They are more expensive in the winter because they are shipped in from other countries, and we have to pay more to do that. What is the price per pound at your grocery store? Can dried fruit be stored longer than fresh fruit? Which is a better buy in summer—grapes or raisins? In winter?

Here's one way:

> SAFETY NOTE: Ask the adults in your home for permission or help whenever you are going to use the oven.

Take 1 pound (0.45 kg) of grapes. Pick them off the stem and place them on a piece of foil on a cookie sheet and dry them in your oven at 250 degrees. Check every 30 minutes to see how the grapes look. Carefully remove them from the oven when they look like raisins to you. Weigh them. How much water did they lose?

What you'll need: Scale, baking sheet, aluminum foil, oven (with your parent's permission, of course), grapes and other fruit.

Have you thought about? Controls: Are red, purple, and green grapes the same?

What did you find out? Data:

Date	Type of Grapes or Fruit	Drying Time	Weight before Drying	Weight after Drying	% Loss

Now, what would happen if? How do other fruits compare with the percentage of water lost in drying? Will apples lose more or less water than grapes? Pears? Apricots? Peaches?

Going to the fair: Have bowls of both fresh and dried fruit and your data on how much water each lost. You can also show samples of dried fruit so that everyone can see what a difference water makes.

MAILBAG

What about? How much junk mail comes to your home?

Find Out About: According to *50 Simple Things You Can Do to Save the Earth*, Americans receive almost 2 million tons (180,000 metric tonnes) of junk mail every year. That's lots of trees. It also says that 44 percent of this mail is never opened. Call your post office and ask about junk mail. How much does it cost to send? How much does the post office process per week?

What's your guess? How much junk mail comes to your home in a week? How much does it weigh? How much junk mail comes to the homes of your friends?

Here's one way: Decide on the length of time you are going to count—the more weeks, the better. Will you count the number of pieces of junk mail or weigh it at the end? Maybe you should consider doing both. What will you count? There will be mail addressed to "current resident," and there will be mail coming to people in your family who didn't ask for it. Both of those types can be considered junk mail. Letters from grandma are not. Unfortunately, bills are not junk mail either.

You can ask friends to count and collect their junk mail, too. You could give them a chart similar to the one below to keep track.

	Monday	Tuesday	Wednesday	Thursday	Friday	Saturday
Week 1						
Week 2						
Week 3						
Week 4						
Week 5						
Week 6						
Total						

Total for all days _____. Which day brings the most junk mail?

Weigh all of the junk mail collected. How does the weight compare with what your friends collected?

Have you thought about the number of trees that must be cut down to make all of that mail?

Going to the fair: Take all of the mail collected. If you have asked other people to collect for you, you may want to have them write over their names and addresses with Magic Marker to protect their privacy. Visitors will be amazed to see how much junk mail there is. After your science fair is over, remember to recycle the mail collected. Remove plastic windows from envelopes.

You can write to the address below to stop having your name sold to most large mailing list companies. If your visitors are interested, you could give them a form to fill out like the one below.

Please remove my name from lists being sold to mailing list companies.
Name_____
Address_____
_____

They can send the form to Mail Preference Service, Direct Marketing Association, 11 West 42nd Street, P.O. Box 3861, New York, NY 10163-3861.

Part Two

IT'S ALL WET

"ALL STEAMED UP"

What about? Have you ever wondered how long it takes for steam to disappear from a mirror after you take a shower or bath? Does the temperature of the air inside the bathroom and the air outside the bathroom have an effect? How would you find out?

What's your guess?

Here's one way: First things first. Record the air temperature inside the bathroom. Record the air temperature outside the bathroom. You may want to make two columns on your paper and label one "Inside Bathroom" and one "Outside Bathroom" so that you won't get confused later. You could set up a chart similar to the one below:

	Inside Bathroom	Outside Bathroom
Starting temperature		
Ending temperature		

Time spent in the shower _____.

Time it takes for steam to disappear from mirror _____.

    Now take your shower. Make sure no one is waiting in line after you. This is scientific research, and it will take some time. (Mothers of the world will be grateful for the added benefit of clean children.) Don't stay in too long. After all we don't want to waste water.

    Is the mirror steamed up? OK, get out, dry off (clothes are optional).

    Now measure the air temperature inside the bathroom. Look at your watch and write down the time. Open the bathroom door. Measure and record the temperature outside the bathroom. Leave the bathroom door open and time how long it takes for the steam to disappear from the mirror.

What you'll need: Watch, pencil and paper, thermometer.

Have you thought about? Controls: Would it take a longer or shorter time if you closed the bathroom door after taking the ending temperature readings? What about taking that shower with the bathroom door open? Would it take longer for steam to form? What about the length of time it would take to disappear?

    How large is your sample size? Will you do this experiment once? Twice? Twenty times?

What did you find out?

    Now, what would happen if? What if the inside temperature and outside temperature were different from what you measured today? What if the humidity were higher or lower? (Is there a weather phone number in your area? If so, that would give you the humidity. There is also a scientific instrument called a hygrometer that is used for measuring humidity. Is there one in your school that you could borrow?) What if the air-conditioning or heat were on in your home?

    Going to the fair: Take your original data. Record keeping is very important. Include a paragraph with background information about your experiment. It's always a good idea to involve the people who are coming to look at your presentation. Have a small mirror and a watch with a second hand. Have a person breathe on the mirror to fog it up. (It's the same principle as your shower experiment.) How long does it take for the moisture to disappear from the mirror? Record the person's name and the results.

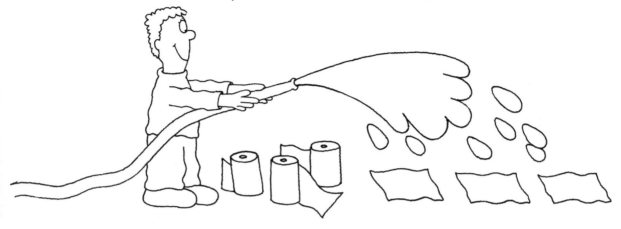

WHICH IS THE "QUICKEST PICKER-UPPER"?

What about? Have you seen or heard commercials that claim that one brand of paper towels is better than another at wiping up spills? Are there differences in absorption rates? How would you find out?

Find out about: Look up *absorption* in a science book or encyclopedia. Ask ten people which brand of paper towel they use and why. Record their answers.

What's your guess?

Here's one way: Use at least three different brands of paper towels. Tear off a sheet of each, measuring to make sure they are the same size. Lay the three sheets side by side on top of a piece of plastic that protects your work surface. Pour 1 oz. (30 ml) of water into the middle of the first piece of paper towel. How long does it take for all of the water to be soaked up (absorbed) into the paper towel? Try the second and third. Is there any difference?

What you'll need: 3 different kinds of paper towels, plastic cover for your work surface, water, measuring cup, watch.

Have you thought about? Is the amount of water the same for each trial? Are the paper towels the same size? Is the table you are working on flat?

What did you find out?

Now, what would happen if you used other brands of paper toweling? If you poured the water onto the plastic first and then put down the towel? If you folded or crumpled the paper toweling? If you varied the water temperature? If you dipped a paper towel into an 8-ounce (0.24-liter) cup of water to see how much of the water the paper towel would absorb?

Going to the fair. Don't forget to take along the survey of which brands of paper towels people you know are using and why. Have your experiment set up to show. Show your research on absorption.

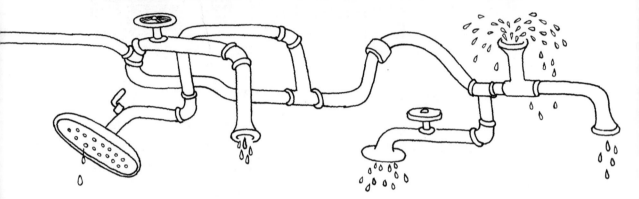

HOW MUCH WATER?

What about? How much water do you use in your home? Think about all the ways you use water—brushing your teeth, taking a bath or shower, washing dishes (you do help with dishes, right?), washing clothes. What other things can you think of that use water in your home? What activities use the most water? Are there ways that you could use less?

What's your guess?

Here are some ways: Do you leave the water running while you brush your teeth? How much water do you use? The next time you brush your teeth, catch and measure any water you use. Try turning the water off until you absolutely need to rinse your mouth and toothbrush. Again, catch the water. How much less water do you use? How could you do that experiment without all the toothpaste mess? Why not try timing the amount of water that collects in a container after 1 minute. How long do you usually brush your teeth?

Date	Amount of Time Allowed for Brushing Teeth	Water Used While Brushing Teeth with Water Running	Water Used While Brushing Teeth with Water on Only When Needed	Difference in Amount of Water Used

What you'll need: toothbrush, toothpaste, container for catching water, watch.

2. Do you take showers or baths? Which use more water? This will be easier to do if your bathtub also has a shower. You could simply plug the tub and take a shower. Is the height of the water higher or lower than you would use to take a bath? How long do you stay in the shower? (The longer you stay in the shower, the more water you use.) How much less water would you use if you cut the time down?

Date	Bathtub— Height of Water	Shower— Height of Water	Length of Time in Shower	Which Uses More Water?

What you'll need: watch, yardstick or meter stick.

Going to the fair: Take your research. Find out how many people take baths and how many take showers. Can you suggest ways in which your visitors can save water?

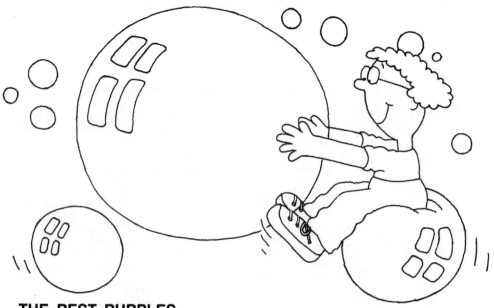

THE BEST BUBBLES

What about? Which dish soaps make the best bubbles?
What's your guess?

Here's one way: Ask your friends (at least ten) which liquid soap they use in their home and why. You could set up a chart similar to this one:

Name of Soap	Good Suds (Bubbles)	Cost	Other

Which dish-washing soaps are the most popular among your friends? Choose the three with the highest marks for suds for your tests. Ask your friends to bring you 1 tablespoon (15 ml) of their soap in a clear container.

Test 1: Set out containers of the same size and shape for each sample you are testing. Add ½ cup (120 ml) water (make sure the temperature is the same for each sample) to each container. Add 1 teaspoon (5 ml) liquid soap. (Use a clean spoon for each sample.) Stir each sample with equal vigor and for equal lengths of time.

Which make the most foam? Measure with a ruler from the bottom of the foam to the top of the foam and record.

Test 2: What if you wanted to use this soapy water for blowing bubbles? Bend a pipe cleaner into a bubble wand. Use a different pipe cleaner for each sample. Dip the wand into the liquid and blow a bubble. Which soapy liquid makes the best bubbles?

Test 3: Which bubble liquid stands up better under greasy conditions? Pour 1 teaspoon (5 ml) vegetable oil into each container. Stir. What happens? Is there any difference among your samples? Measure the height of the foam in each container now.

What you'll need: Several different kinds of dish-washing liquid, clean clear containers (the same size and shape) for each dish-washing liquid), a clean spoon for each kind of dish-washing liquid, a teaspoon measure, a pipe cleaner for each dish-washing liquid, 1 teaspoon (5 ml) vegetable oil for each sample, water, a ruler.

Have you thought about? Controls: What will happen if you use hot water instead of cool water? What will happen if you use 2 teaspoons (10 ml) of soap instead of 1?

Going to the fair: Take your survey. In fact, you could ask your visitors which dish-washing soap they use. Set up your tests.

"IT'S ALL WET!"

What about? Does wool or cotton cloth hold more water?

Why does it matter? Will you ever want to buy or wear a piece of clothing made of cotton or wool (or even mostly cotton or wool)? Will it matter to you if you get caught in the rain? Which fabric holds less water and will dry out faster?

Did you know? Fabrics are used for much more than making clothes. Some of the people in Mongolia live in wool felt tents, called *yurts*, which they can roll up and move when they want to change their living place. For research, you can find out more about these people. You can also find out when people started to use each of these types of cloth and maybe even something about how they are made.

What's your guess? Do equal-size pieces of cotton and wool cloth hold the same amount of water?

Here's one way: Measure and cut pieces of 100% cotton and 100% wool about 1 foot (30 cm) square. Weigh each piece dry on a scale that measures grams and parts of grams. Write down the weights. Lower the fabrics into a bowl of water; then hold them up and let the extra water drip off. Weigh them again. Write down the weights. Subtract the first weight from the second. Which fabric held more water?

What you'll need: Pieces of 100% cotton and wool, gram scale, bowl, water, pencil, paper.

Have you thought about? Controls: Cotton cloth and wool cloth can each be woven in heavy or light weights. Does it make a difference if you are measuring heavy cloth in one fabric and light cloth in another?

What did you find out? Data: Try the different types of fabric and write down the results, using the chart below as an example. Under "Absorption Rating," put down "1" for the fabric that absorbed the most water, "2" for the next most absorbent, and so on.

Fabric Type	Dry Weight	Wet Weight	Absorption Rating

Now, what would happen if? Many fabrics are part wool, part cotton, part nylon or polyester, or many other kinds of things. How much change is there in the amount of water a fabric can carry or absorb when it is mixed with another fabric?

Going to the fair: A display on water absorption of different fabrics could be quite colorful. This is a simple experiment, and you could have your whole setup at the table and ask people to predict and try different pieces right there.

A HIGHER GLASS OF WATER

What about? How much water does a glass hold? We usually talk about juice glasses, water glasses, wine glasses, teacups, mugs, and more. We have pictures in our minds about what shape and how large these glasses and cups are. Sodas are sold by size. The small, medium, and large cups have a certain number of ounces or liters. The containers can't be full because then they might spill. Just how full can you fill a container?

Did you know? The top of your liquid in the container is called the *meniscus* (min-is-kiss). If it is just over the rim, it is *convex*. If it is under the rim, it is *concave*. Can you guess why we see these different phenomena? See if you can find out the reason. (Hint: Look up "surface tension.") Lenses are also convex and concave, and they change the way you see things. You can use a drop of water as a lens because it curves. Try it and see what happens. (Hint: You'll need to put your drop on top of a piece of plastic, waxed paper, or glass so that it doesn't soak into whatever you're trying to look at.)

What's your guess? Will the height of your meniscus (and the amount of water in a container) change with different sizes of containers?

Why does it matter? When is "full" really full? Would you rather have a full glass that's tall and narrow or one that's short and wide? Is there a difference?

Here's one way: Gather several round containers of different heights and widths. Measure their diameters (a straight line across at the widest point) and fill them to the top with water. Pour the water from one into a measuring cup and record the amount. Pour it back into the container. Then, with an eye dropper, a pipette, or a straw, begin to drip water into that full container slowly. Keep adding water until the first bit drips over. Measure this new amount in your measuring cup again. Do this for each container. Do you lose any water when you pour back and forth from container to measuring cup?

What you'll need: a variety of containers, water, clear glass measuring cup, eye dropper or pipette (a straw can work well too).

Have you thought about? Controls: Are all of your containers made of the same material (glass, plastic, metal)? Will it make a difference?

What did you find out? Data:

Type of Container	Diameter	Height	"Full" Amount	Amount with Meniscus built up

Now, what would happen if? Is there any change in these amounts if you use liquids other than water? Do solids like sugar and flour do the same thing?

Going to the fair: Ask your visitors to take part. Set up a display with a number of containers and let them try to guess how much extra water can be added to a container that already looks full.

Part Three

MAKING CHANGE

A BETTER LOAF

What about? How can you get the most rising out of yeast in your bread?

Did you know? Bread is one of the oldest of prepared human foods. There are forms of bread in almost every culture. You find tortillas and bagels and brioches and pancakes on the tables of different people all over the world. Do you know of other breads from other parts of the world?

What's your guess? Does yeast work better with cold, warm, or hot water? With sugar or without? With honey? Syrup? Flour?

Why does it matter? Bread is delicious and nutritious when it's baked well. Doing this experiment will let you experience a better bread.

Here's one way: Use three tall clear glasses. Fill them half full of water at three different temperatures. Use a thermometer to record the temperatures on a chart. Add ¼ teaspoon of active granular yeast to each glass and stir. Measure the foam caps (the

foam that forms on top of the liquid mixture) every 5 minutes for half an hour. Pour everything out and wash the glasses. Start again, but this time add one other item, such as flour, sugar, or honey, in measured amounts. Watch, measure, and record what happens.

What you'll need: 3 tall clear glasses, water, cooking thermometer, active yeast, flour, sugar.

Have you thought about? Controls: Are all of your glasses the same size and shape? Does your measuring method keep everything equal? Is all of your "laboratory equipment" starting at the same temperature?

What did you find out? Data:

Height of Foam after This Many Minutes

Temperature	5	10	15	20	25	30
Temp 1						
Temp 2						
Temp 3						

Now, what would happen if? If you didn't spill the yeast out after the experiment time and just let it keep growing, what would happen? What would happen if a bread stayed out a long time rising before it was baked?

Going to the fair:

Safety Note:

Use an oven only with permission and supervision of your parents, of course.

Bake several loaves of bread. You can use the recipe here or another simple yeast bread. Keep the rising times the same, but change the amounts of yeast and the temperatures. Display the samples at your table with the data from your experiments.

Bread recipe:
1 Cup warm water (105–115 degrees F)
1 Tablespoon margarine
1 Tablespoon sugar
1 Tablespoon salt
1 Package active yeast
3½ Cups flour (you might need a little more or less depending on how humid a day it is)

Mix the warm water with the yeast, sugar, ½ cup of flour, and margarine until it is all combined well. Slowly add enough flour until you can work with the dough and it is no longer sticky. On a wet day, your flour takes in more moisture, and you will need more flour than on a dry day. Put the dough in a bowl, rub a little cooking oil all over the top to prevent it from drying out, and cover it with a clean dish towel. When it rises to about double its original size (about 1 hour), punch it down and put it into two loaf pans (9×5×3 inches [22.5×12.5×7.5 cm]). Or you can divide the dough in half and make braids or other fancy shapes. Cover the bread with your clean towel again and let it rise until it is double again. Preheat your oven (with parent help) to 350 degrees and bake the bread dough about 45 minutes or until the loaf is golden brown and sounds hollow when you tap it.

For your experiment display, you could bake the loaves using different temperatures of water with the yeast. You could also use different amounts of sugar and yeast. Cut the loaves open to show the differences.

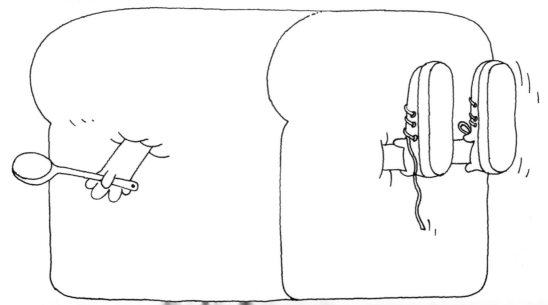

MORE ON BREAD

What about? You can have a lot more on bread than jam or peanut butter. Bread is a great place to grow molds. Some breads are "natural" and have no preservatives to keep them fresh. Other breads have chemicals added to them to keep away the molds for a while. How well do they work?

Did you know? The scientific name of what we call "bread mold" is *Rhizopus stolonifer.* It starts out looking like white cotton, but as it grows it gets black speckles. There are other kinds of molds that can grow on a piece of bread. Before you know it, you can have a colorful mold garden! Big bakeries that sell bread in many stores often add the chemical calcium propionate to the recipe to keep the bread from spoiling.

What's your guess? How long does calcium propionate keep the mold away?

Why does it matter? Would you eat up the loaf of bread before it would spoil anyway? Do you want to buy your bread with or without chemicals?

Here's one way: Take two pieces of bread bought fresh on the same day. One piece of bread should be without a chemical preservative; the other should have it. Check the labels to make sure, or ask the bakeries.

Put each piece in a clean new plastic bag and close the bag. This gives you a control of the space around each piece of bread and also keeps the moisture in, which will speed the molding process.

Observe the pieces each day. When does the mold appear on each one?

Have you thought about? Controls: Are the breads of the same type—that is, are you using white bread, whole wheat, rye, or another kind? Is the temperature the same for both? Are they the same size?

What did you find out? Data:

	White Bread with Preservatives	White Bread without Preservatives	Rye with Preservatives	Rye without Preservatives
Day 1				
Day 2				
Day 3				
etc. . .				

Now, what would happen if? Would there be any difference if the breads were a different type? If you tried white bread, do you think whole wheat bread or pumpernickel would mold more quickly or more slowly than the white?

Does temperature make a difference? Would mold appear more quickly or more slowly if you placed the bread slices in the refrigerator? What if the bread is toasted? How long does the mold continue to grow if you don't throw the bread away when it begins?

Going to the fair: You can have bread samples, mold samples, and questions for your visitors: How long has this mold been growing? For plain bread? For whole wheat? For rye? For pumpernickel?

You can have bread wrappers with a list of the ingredients. Which bread would your visitors choose to buy and why? (This sounds like the beginning of another experiment.)

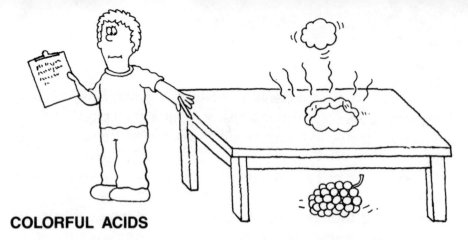

COLORFUL ACIDS

What about? Do you drink orange juice? Do you take vitamin C? Do you eat sour pickles? These sour things contain a kind of chemical known as an *acid*. These acids are weak enough to eat or drink. There are also acids in your stomach to help break down the food you eat. Some acids are so dangerous that they can burn your skin or dissolve glass.

Have you heard of antacids? A TV commercial may tell you to take a particular antacid to reduce the acid in your stomach. Can you think of any antacids that you have seen advertised (Maalox, milk of magnesia, Di-Gel, Alka-Seltzer)? Another antacid that you may have in your kitchen is baking soda. Many commercial antacids contain baking soda (sodium bicarbonate). These antacids are also known as "bases."

In this project you will use colorful acids such as grape juice and cranberry juice along with baking soda and water to make colorful tie-dyed creations. What happens when you add baking soda dissolved in water to a piece of fabric that has been dyed in a colorful fruit juice?

What's your guess?

Find out about: Acids and bases. What do they do? What happens when you add an acid to a base?

Test some old white scrap fabric. Pieces of old sheets or men's white handkerchiefs are good. Dye a piece of fabric with cranberry juice and let it dry. Make a solution of baking soda and water, using about 1 teaspoon baking soda to ¼ cup water. Dribble the baking soda solution in a pattern on the fabric you dyed with cranberry juice. What happens? Repeat your experiment on another piece of fabric, using grape juice for the dye. What happens when you use the baking soda first and then add a colored juice? To keep track of the color changes you could set up a chart as follows:

Liquid Used to Dye Fabric	Liquid Dribbled On	Color Change If Any
1.		
2.		
3.		

After you have achieved results you like, try tie-dyeing an old white or light-colored T-shirt.

Have you thought about? What will happen when you wash your juice and baking-soda-dyed fabric? Will the color stay in when it's washed?

Going to the fair: Take along samples of the fabrics you dyed. Don't forget your chart.

Another investigation: Acid rain is in the news a lot these days. Acid rain occurs when rain and chemicals from car exhaust or factory smoke combine to form an acid. Sometimes this acid is very harmful to plants and animals and bodies of water. You might be interested in collecting rainwater and testing it with a special paper called litmus paper. Litmus paper is specially treated to show whether a liquid is an acid or a base.

"X" MARKS THE SPOT

What about? What happens in your home if you get a huge spot of ketchup on your brand-new shirt? What are your options? Dye the shirt? Get the spot out? Add more spots so that you will have a polka dot shirt? Add it to the ragbag?

What's your guess? If you try to wash the stain out, which laundry detergent works best?

Did you know? People have been making and using soaps for thousands of years. Soap works by being able to lift and hold dirt particles until they can be washed away. We often use the words *soap* and *detergent* to mean the same thing. They work in much the same way but are made by different methods. Soaps are made from fat and chemicals called *alkalis.* Long ago in this country people made soap by first pouring hot water over wood ashes to make potash and then boiling the potash with animal fat in large iron kettles. Detergents were developed in the early 1900s. They use synthetic (people-made) chemicals to lift and hold the dirt particles. Detergents work better than soaps in *hard* water, which is water that contains mineral deposits. Check the labels on the products you are testing to see whether you are testing soaps or detergents.

Here's one way: Take a survey of the people you know. Set up a chart so that you can keep track of the results. It could look something like this:

Name	What stains are toughest for you to clean?	Name of soap or detergent	Is this soap or detergent liquid or powder?	Why was soap or detergent chosen?	Rate of cleaning power (1 to 5, with 5 being the best)	How long has person used this brand?

How many people will you ask? Ask your science teacher what a reasonable sample size would be.

How many of the brands named in your survey will you test?
Will you test only powdered detergents, only liquids or both?
Will you test only detergents, only soaps or both?
What kind(s) of fabric will you test? What size fabric will you use?
What stain(s) will you test?
How will you measure the amount of stain that you put on each fabric sample?
What water temperature will you use?
Will you hand-wash your fabric or use a washing machine?
Will you use a clothes dryer or line-dry your fabric?
How can you make sure that you do the exact same thing to each sample?

What did you find out? Data: One way to show your results clearly is by setting up a chart.

Controls

Water temperature
Kind of fabric used
Size of fabric
Method of washing
Method of drying
Method of rating stain removal: 1 to 5, with 5 being the best

Name of Stains

Detergent Names	Stain 1	Stain 2	Stain 3	Etc.
Detergent 1				
Detergent 2				
Detergent 3				
Etc.				

What you'll need: Several brands of laundry detergent or soap, several pieces of fabric, several stains, water, washing machine or dishpan.

Another consideration: Read about how soaps and detergents affect the environment. How can we balance the need to clean things with the need to keep our lakes and streams healthy?

Going to the fair: Make sure you take along your original data. Display various samples of the fabrics you tested. Let viewers stain and test samples if that is possible.

A COAT OF PAINT

What about? Are different paints equally as good on a piece of wood?

Did you know? Pigments (colorings) for paint color come from many places. Some are made from plants, like the *indigo* dyes used to color jeans. Some dyes come from minerals, like the red that appears when iron rusts. And some come from animals, like the old-fashioned brown ink called *sepia*, which comes from a sea animal.

What's your guess? What will happen to different types of paint when they are brushed on a piece of wood and the wood is left

outside in sun, rain, heat, and cold? This is called "weathering" because the material is left out in whatever weather happens.

Why does it matter? Paint is a form of protective coating. When you paint a house, a toy, or any other project, you want to know if the paint will, in fact, protect and last.

Here's one way: See if you have or can buy at least three types of paint at a hardware or hobby store. There are latex paints, oil paints, watercolors, tempera paints, finger paints, and more. Take one large board (about 6 inches by 24 inches [15 cm × 60 cm]) and mark it into sections. Or use smaller pieces of board, one for each type of paint. Paint the pieces with one coat, or layer, of paint. Set them in a sunny, dry place. Observe them closely once a week for two or more months. Take pictures if you can.

What you'll need: three or more paints, paint brushes, a large wooden board or small pieces of one kind of wood.

Have you thought about? Controls: Are all the paints the same color? Will different colors (pigments in the paint) change the experiment? Are your wood pieces all the same? Are they all exposed to the same weather?

What did you find out? Data:

	Paint 1	Paint 2	Paint 3
Dates/ observations			

Now, what would happen if? What would you predict if you used one type of your paint on different surfaces, such as plastic or metal?

Going to the fair: Take your wood pieces, your containers of paint, and any drawings or photographs. Set them up and ask your visitors to guess what paints gave you which results.

TURNING BROWN BEFORE YOUR EYES

What about? Have you ever cut an apple or banana into slices and had them turn an unappetizing brown color before your eyes? Why does this happen and how can it be prevented?

What's your guess?

Here's one way: Ask several people which fruits and/or vegetables turn brown after they are peeled and/or sliced. How do they keep these foods from turning brown? Do they add lemon juice, cover potatoes with water, or use some other method?

Name of Vegetable or Fruit	Method of Preservation

After you have completed your survey, take the top three vegetables or fruits that your survey found to be problems and the three top-rated methods of keeping them from turning brown. How will you find out if one method is best for most problem fruits and vegetables? Another consideration: Will what you use change the taste of the fruit or vegetable? Test each food using each method. You could set up a chart something like this:

Name of Food	Method 1	Method 2	Method 3	Notes
1.				
2.				
3.				

Don't forget to describe in detail each preservation method. You can use the Notes section of the chart to state whether any of the methods altered the taste of the food or for any other comments.

Have you thought about? Do different varieties of each fruit or vegetable that you are testing react differently to your methods of keeping them from turning dark? For instance, do Macintosh apples differ from Granny Smith or Golden Delicious apples in how quickly they turn dark? Does the same method of preservation work equally well for all kinds of apples? Does it matter whether you use a plastic knife or metal knife for cutting the fruit or other food?

Going to the fair: Take along your original survey. Display samples of treated and untreated fruit and/or vegetables.

Part Four

PEOPLE PROJECTS

"IN THE PINK"

What about? Do people see the same color at the same time?

Did you know? Your eye sends messages about what it sees to the brain through the optic nerve, the way a wire carries electricity. At the back of your eye are *rods and cones*, parts of your body that can see color. These don't work well in some people, and such people are said to be "color-blind."

What's your guess? Will boys see differently from girls? Will teachers see differently from students?

Why does it matter? If people see things differently, then maybe they are not seeing what you want them to see when you do your display.

Here's one way: Cut up one sheet of pink construction paper into five pieces. Put each of those pieces on a larger piece of different background color. Will people say that the pink pieces are different shades?

Have you thought about? Controls: Are your pink pieces and background pieces the same size? Will you show them to people in the same room lighting or outdoors?

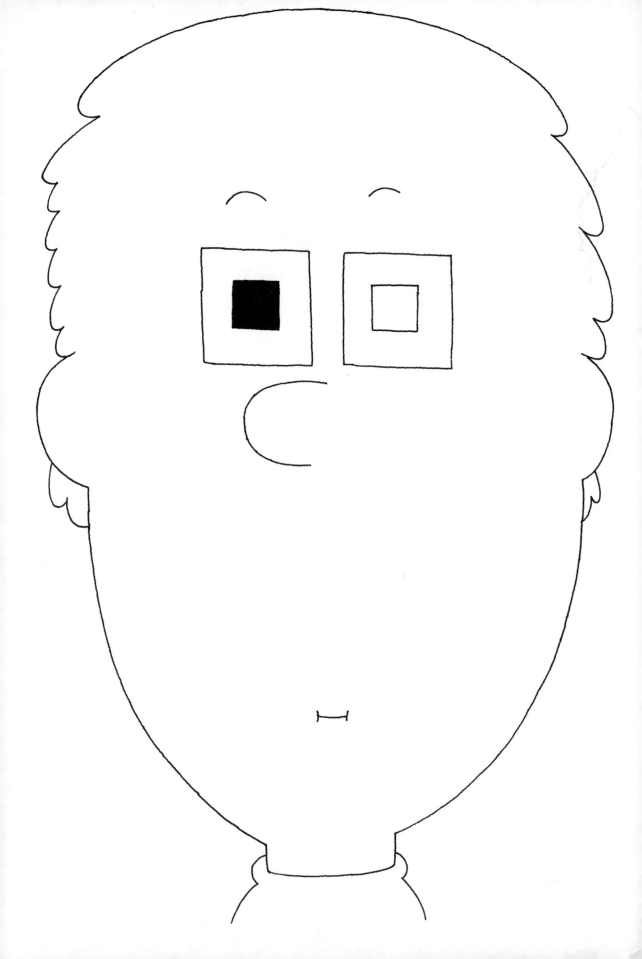

What did you find out? Data:

Number of Colors Identified (1–5)

Girls	Boys	Male Teachers	Female Teachers

Now, what would happen if? Is the same true with other colors? Does it matter if the color is dark or light?

Going to the fair: Put your data under a cover on the display so that visitors can't see what you found out until you are ready to show them. Put your experiment up on display and ask people to add to your data. Then let them peek at what you've already found out!

FOOT AND FOREARM SURVEY

What about? How does the length of your foot compare to the length of your forearm? Are they the same length? Is it possible for you to go into a shoe store and say, "I need a shoe the size of my forearm"? What about other people?

What's your guess? Is the length of the forearm the same as the length of the foot in most people?

Here's one way: Measure the length of your foot. Measure the length of your forearm. Here's the trick: You have to decide whether to measure your forearm from the inside of the elbow to your wrist

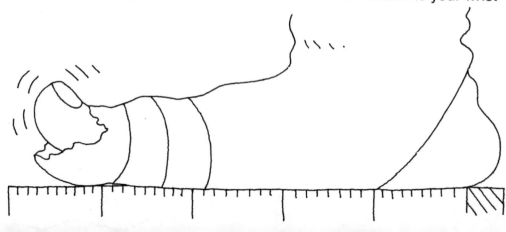

or take the outside measurement. The outside is longer, of course. You have to decide whether to measure your foot from your heel to your big toe, your middle toe, or to your longest or shortest toe. Once you have these controls, you can test your hypothesis.

Have you thought about whether a person's age has anything to do with whether the two measurements are similar?

Set up a chart similar to the one below:

Name	Fore-arm Length	Foot Length	Baby under 2 Years	Ages 2 to 10	Ages 10 to 15	Ages 15 to 20	Over 21

What did you find out?

Going to the fair: Take your original work. Show any age difference if you found any. Take a tape measure along with you so that your visitors can try your experiment.

THE "NOSE KNOWS," OR DOES IT?

What about? What are your favorite smells? What are your favorite tastes? Are they the same? What happens to your appetite when you have a cold and your nose is all stopped up and you can't

smell anything? How does smell affect taste? What will happen if you close your eyes and have someone place one food under your nose and a different food in your mouth?

What's your guess? How does smell affect taste?

Here's one way: Peel and cut into bite-size chunks an apple and a raw potato. Make sure that the sizes are approximately the same size. Put on a blindfold and ask a friend to hold one of the food items under your nose and then place the other in your mouth. Can you guess which food is in your mouth? Does it make a difference which food is placed under the nose? Ask your friend to be the tester (subject). Place the apple piece under friend's nose and the potato in your friend's mouth. Can he/she guess? Reverse the foods and try again.

Would it make a difference if you didn't know which two foods were being used? Try an onion and a apple. Keep a record of your testing. Test other people. How many should you test?

Your test chart could look something like the one below: Fill in the sex and age of the person being tested. Place a check for each time the person guessed correctly what was placed in his/her mouth.

Male/ Female	Age	Apple/ Nose Potato/ Mouth	Potato/ Nose Apple/ Mouth	Apple/ Nose Onion/ Mouth	Onion/ Nose Apple/ Mouth
1.					
2.					
3.					
4.					

Have you thought about? Are there any differences in your test results between boys and girls? Men and women? Children and adults? Older people?

Going to the fair: Take your original records. This is the perfect kind of test to do with the people who attend the science fair, and you will be adding to your records.

LEFT HAND, RIGHT HAND

What about? Are you left-handed or right-handed? What about your friends? What about the kids and the teachers in your school? How would you go about finding out?

What's your guess? What percentage of the people in your school are right-handed? Is it the same for males and females? Children and adults?

Here's one way: You never know until you ask. To keep track of what people say, set up a chart. It might be interesting to keep a record of the sex of the people and the approximate age. (Don't forget that some adults are very sensitive about their age. Be sensitive and don't pry too much.)

Person	Right-handed	Left-handed	Male	Female	5–10 yrs	10–20 yrs	20 yrs +
1.							
2.							
3.							
4.							
5.							
6.							
7.							
8.							

The sample chart has spaces for only eight people. You will want to ask many more people. The more you ask, the more accurate your results will be.

Analyzing your results: You are looking at a lot of different things in your survey. You want to know how many females are right-handed and how many are left-handed. You have also asked about age. How can you get all of this information to make sense? You could simply look at the total number of people that you ask and count the number of left-handed people and right-handed people. You can turn that into a percentage by dividing the number of right-handed people by the total number of people asked. You can do the same for left-handed people.

If you want to get more complicated, you can look at the number of right-handed females compared to the number of right-handed males. You can further complicate this if you get into the ages of the people you ask. You decide. You can keep it simple or get into a lot of detail.

Have you thought about? What is the national average for numbers of left- and right-handed people? How would you go about finding out? How does our country compare with other countries?

Going to the fair: Display your results, and as long as you're there, get more. Ask your visitors whether they are right-handed or left-handed.

MATCHING GENES?

What about? Do more people with black hair have brown eyes? Do most people with blond hair have blue eyes?

Did you know? Gregor Mendel (1822–1884) was a monk who lived in Austria. He wanted to know more about how plants grew in

size and shape. He planted peas in the garden and labeled them. When they were grown, he carefully collected their seeds. He kept data on the tall and short plants and the smooth and wrinkled ones. He saw that the way they grew up depended on their parent plants. He played an important part in the beginning of the study of *genetics.* It wasn't until the early 1900s, after Mendel had died, that other scientists understood how important his work was.

What's your guess? Do you think hair color and eye color are inherited together or separately?

Why does it matter? It is interesting to see how families look alike. Much of this is due to traits like hair and eye color, passed from parents to children. Do certain traits stay together, and is that why families tend to look alike?

Here's one way: Prepare a chart like the one below and then just look at people and mark down what you find. You can use your mathematics skills to figure out what percentage of people have the same eye and hair colors. Be polite and explain what you're doing so that your classmates don't think you're staring because there's a problem!

Have you thought about? Controls: How will you mark down "almost brown" for blonds or "almost black" for dark brown hair? What about people with hazel or mixed eye colors?

What did you find out? Data:

	Brown Hair	Black Hair	Red Hair	Blond Hair
Black eyes				
Brown eyes				
Blue eyes				
Green eyes				
Hazel eyes				

Now, what would happen if? The data collection above doesn't separate boys and girls or adults from children. What would happen if you tried to compare these different groups. Would your results change?

Going to the fair: This is one hypothesis that you can continue to collect data on at the fair. You can explain what you did on your display, and you can also have lots of pictures of friends and family. Ask your visitors to think about how traits are passed from one generation to the next.

A SCIENCE FAIR
IS ONLY THE BEGINNING

The science fair and your project in it give you a quick look into the world of science. We hope you have fun planning your project, doing it, and telling others about it. Most of the projects in this book come from questions about the things all around you. A science fair is a great way to get going, but you don't need a science fair to wonder about how your world works.

If you like doing experiments and thinking like a scientist, here are a few things you can do for yourself:

1. The best thing you can do for yourself is to find a "mentor." A mentor is someone who is working at science and who will take the time to share your interest in it. Your mentor could be a teacher in your school, a professor at a nearby college, an older friend, or an adult who does science for work or as a hobby. Don't be afraid to say that you'd like to talk about science or tag along and see what they do. You can even offer to help out.

2. Visit a science museum. The job of the people at a museum is to show and explain things to you. There are often scientists working behind the scenes at museums, in parks, and other places where science is part of the exhibits. Many museums are free or have reduced rates for students. Find out where the nearest museums are and see what they've got.

3. At your local library you can learn from people who wrote things down thousands of years ago. Your librarian knows a lot

about which books have what information. He'll know which ones are easy or hard to read for you if you tell him what you like. There are also films, tapes, and picture files that your library may lend.

4. Practice. Thinking is a skill, like playing the piano or batting a home run. When you see something that interests you, think about how you would set up an experiment to prove or disprove your judgment. This can be lots of fun. How often does your brother knock on your door before he enters? Does your father often smile when he says a certain word? What happens to leftovers in your refrigerator? How much is thrown out and how much is served at another meal? How much paper is used at your school? What are the ways it could be recycled?

Science often leads to inventions. Human beings have always invented things. We are good at that. Some people think that inventing is what makes us different from other animals. Do you like to invent little ways to do things more easily or in a new way? Sometimes it's fun just to sit and think about how something might be done. This is the creative part of science. A scientist needs to create or invent an experiment that will be really convincing to other scientists. An inventor starts with things that become pieces of something new.

If your project is interesting, but you need more supplies or money than you have to get it done, you can often find help just by asking a mentor. There's an old saying, "Nothing ventured, nothing gained." Many people at your school are there to help you, but they may not know how if you don't tell them what you need. Don't be shy. Don't give up too easily. Science is fun, and you can do it!

FOR FURTHER READING

For other project ideas you might take a look at some of these books:

Agler, Leigh. *Liquid Explorations*. Berkeley: University of California, Lawrence Hall of Science, 1987.

Allison, Linda, and David Katz. *Gee Whiz*. Calif.: Yolla Bolly Press, 1983.

Barber, Jacqueline. *Vitamin Testing*. Berkeley: University of California, Lawrence Hall of Science, 1988.

Brown, Robert J. *333 Science Tricks and Experiments*. Blue Ridge Summit, Pa.: TAB Books, 1984.

Brown, Robert. *200 Illustrated Science Experiments for Children*. Blue Ridge Summit, Pa.: TAB Books, 1987.

Burns, Marilyn. *The I Hate Mathematics Book*. Boston: Little, Brown, 1975.

Caney, Steven. *Steven Caney's Playbook*. New York: Workman, 1975.

Caney, Steven. *Steven Caney's Invention Book*. New York: Workman, 1985.

Cobb, Vicki. *Chemically Active*. New York: J. B. Lippincott, 1985.

Cobb, Vicki. *How to Really Fool Yourself*. New York: J. B. Lippincott, 1981.

Donev, Mary, and Stef and Carold Grold. *Food Works*. Toronto: Kids Can Press, 1986.

EarthWorks Group. *50 Simple Things You Can Do to Save the Earth*. Berkeley, Calif.: Earthworks Press, 1989.

Herbert, Don. *Mr. Wizard's Supermarket Science*. New York: Random House, 1980.

Katz, Phyllis. *Exploring Science Through Art*. New York: Franklin Watts, 1990.

McCormack, Alan. *Inventors' Workshop*. Belmont, Calif.: David Lake Publishers, 1981.

McGill, Ormond. *Science Magic, 101 Experiments You Can Do*. New York: Arco, 1984.

Macauley, David. *How Things Work*. Boston: Houghton Mifflin, 1988.

700 Science Experiments for Everyone, compiled by UNESCO. New York: Doubleday, rev. ed. 1964.

Sneider, Cary, and Jacqueline Barber. *Paper Towel Testing*. Berkeley: University of California, Lawrence Hall of Science, 1987.

Stein, Sara. *The Science Book*. New York: Workman, 1979.

Thomas Edison Book of Easy and Incredible Experiments. New York: John Wiley & Sons, 1988.

Watson, Philip. *Liquid Magic*. New York: Lothrop, Lee and Shepard, 1982.

Watson, Philip. *Light Fantastic*. New York: Lothrop, Lee and Shepard, 1982.

Zubrowski, Bernie. *Drinking Straw Construction*. Boston: Little, Brown, 1981.

INDEX

ABOUT THE AUTHORS

Phyllis Katz is the Executive Director of the Hands-on Science Program, an informal after-school program for children (ages 4–12) that emphasizes awareness of "science in your life." The program is based in Rockville, Maryland and serves communities throughout the United States. A New York native and former English teacher, Phyllis lives in Silver Spring, Maryland with her husband, Victor, a mathematics professor, and their three children Sharon, Ari, and Naomi.

Janet Frekko, a former science teacher, is Associate Director of the Hands-on Science Program. She is a North Carolina native who now lives in Rockville, Maryland with her husband, Gene, an electrical engineer, and their two daughters Susan and Karen.